# Conscious Mindful Leadership

Second Edition

**Heather Good**

*all the Best !*
*Heather .*

# Dedication

This book is dedicated to the expansion of love, compassion, and kindness in all people and amongst all communities and workplaces in the world.

A heart-felt thanks to all those people who contributed to the production, design and completion of this book. Thank you to all the talented photographers who submitted their work for this book. Thank you to all my wonderful friends and to Emily Young, Connie Chan, Kim Yarmuch, Kelly Hyde, John Ferguson, Kristie Pshyk, Denise Mikesh, Mom and Dad, Chris Hammer, Renee Toker, and Christine Leinweber for being generous with your time, talents, support, and encouragement.

Deep appreciation is also extended to the Center for Right Relationship founders Faith Fuller and Marita Fridjhon for the development and design of the Organizational and Relationship Systems Coaching program. It is making a significant, positive impact by bringing forth the values of deep democracy and wisdom to organizations around the world.

# Table of Contents

# Introduction

Drawing upon research and literature in the areas of attachment, emotional intelligence, mindfulness and coaching, Conscious Mindful Leadership (CML) assists leaders to become increasingly insightful, to have greater relatedness with others, and to experience fulfillment as a leader.

Many of our responses and behaviours occur automatically and subconsciously. In order to respond effectively as a leader, one must become aware of patterns of behaviour and responses that are creating connection and cohesion and those that are creating difficulties and disconnection.

In order to address the current challenges of working and leading, today's leader must be in tune with the needs of employees, to be able to listen and understand, support, encourage, and provide the kind of stability and inspiration that directs others forward. People want to be in positive environments and surrounded by those who are passionate about what they do. As a leader it is your job to take personal responsibility for your own relationships, to do your part to build a sense of community, and consider the well-being of our planet in your actions. As each one of us takes on this mission, we will collectively experience a positive shift towards health and well-being.

While working as a mental health therapist and leadership educator, I have met many people who report feeling stressed, overwhelmed, isolated and uninspired. Because of this there, is a great need for leaders and managers to be cognizant of the emotional climate of their employees and workplaces. Furthermore, the new four letter word of this generation is "busy." Being busy prevents inner and outer connection and peace of mind. When we are running full out, we lose touch with what brings us passion and vitality, and we become ungrounded, unhappy and egocentric.

I have found in my own life that I tend to thrive on busyness and I love connecting, socializing, and engaging with others. Because I love doing these things, I sometimes neglect my need for quiet time, yoga and meditation. When I am grounded, I am much more in tune with my environment and I am able to ride the ups and downs of life in a calm way: life becomes much easier! With clarity of focus, I become much more capable of leading my own life and more in tune with how to assist others.

Although leadership is a complex, extensively discussed topic, the majority of literature that explores effective leadership does not delve deeply into the intersecting influences of early family relationships, attachment, and relationship style on leadership potential and ability.

In order to be an outstanding leader, self reflection and mindfulness are crucial. Summarizing a study by the Gallup Management Group, David Conchie (2008) noted that self-awareness is one of the top factors in effective leadership as it assists leaders to be in tune with themselves and with others. Although self-awareness is essential to effective leadership, its importance is often overlooked or viewed as inconsequential.

In the following chapters you will have the opportunity to investigate what brings you fulfillment and to explore whether you currently bring your best self forward when dealing with others. In the first half of the book, you will gain insight into what values are driving you at work and what causes your responses in times of conflict. By having the courage to ask questions about what others think of you as a leader, you will learn about some of your blind-spots which may be preventing connection and efficacy. The latter half of the book addresses how you can bring the knowledge you have learned to your team. Some information on the dynamics of teams is shared to support you in understanding toxic behaviours that pull teams down. The final chapter of the book provides exercises which can be practiced anytime to help you gain clarity in your life and in your leadership.

It is through the power of **reflection** that we clearly **see** who we are

Photo by C. Toews

# Historical Overview of Leadership - What Employees Need Now

Over the years, leadership has been influenced by modernization, globalization, changes in markets and technology, downsizing/outsourcing, and even a global recession. In the past, leadership focused on hierarchy and stoicism in the workplace. Rigid, hierarchical, and traditional managers and work environments may have kept employees fearing for their positions. In today's more competitive market, employees move more often between and within organizations and are less likely to tolerate abuse, criticism, or being treated in a condescending manner. In addition, employees are looking for a sense of purpose, connection and job satisfaction. Today's employees look for workplaces that are supportive and healthy.

Due to the changing work culture and the needs of an inter-generational workforce, it is important to ensure that a positive and supportive work environment is developed to assist people in feeling valued and appreciated. Randstad, the second largest provider of staffing services in the world, found that there is a distinct difference between the needs of employees in the different generations. In a 2008 survey, it was found that 16.8% of people in the Canadian workforce were born between the years of 1980 and 1988. This group, sometimes known as Generation Y, responds to leadership by being collaborative and generally multitasks with ease. A second group of individuals, born between 1965 and 1979, often referred to as Generation X, make up 29.2% of the workforce and tend to display competence, general adaptability, independence, self-reliance and pragmatic thinking. The Baby Boomers, born between 1946 and 1964, make up 41.3% of the workforce and are service as well as team oriented and are driven by the need for personal satisfaction. People in the "mature" category, born between 1900 and 1945, make up 12.7 % of the workforce and are generally familiar with hierarchy in organizations as well as being dedicated, hard-working, stable, and patient (Randstad, 2008).

Many examples from our own lives and from occurrences around the world can be described as situations where we look to that other person to change, to be different, to give us what we want, and mostly, to stop being difficult. In fact, some organizational change strategists suggest that if a company employs people who do not share their values they should be removed from the organization. This, however, could be viewed as "throwing in the towel", and although it may seem as if this strategy will solve the problem there can be negative effects such as scapegoating and fear of sharing an opinion that may be different from the norm.

Feelings of helplessness often lead to finger-pointing and blame, and we thus relate to others as either obstacles or supporters in our endeavors to reach our goals. When this happens, we create a disconnection between ourselves and others. Additionally, although we may say we are committed to peace and cooperation, we become angry out of frustration and disempowered because things do not go as we had planned.

Given the complexity of leading different types of people with very different values, it is of the utmost importance that leaders support, understand, listen to, and appreciate each and every employee for their uniqueness. Leaders from all walks of life are being called upon to support employees as not only managers or leaders but as visionaries. Sometimes it is difficult to be an inspiring leader; even with good intentions leaders can become frustrated, burned out, and unsure how to assist others with challenges. Self-reflection and mindfulness practices will assist you in recognizing your own internal signals and those of others, thus, enabling you to be in tune with your environment and with yourself.

As leaders
we accomplish great things with
strength and grace

Photo by T. Capistrano

# Today's Effective Leaders

Your perspective, the intentions you create, and how you choose to interact with others influence your effectiveness as a leader.

Effective leaders have a number of qualities in common: they realize that the bigger the vision, the bigger the outcome, and they are clear in their vision and how to implement it. Great leaders are in tune with their own unique leadership talents and they are able to assist others to recognize their own talents. In addition, they explore the definition of success; they know how to develop a team they can trust and they ensure that they match people's strengths, talents, knowledge, and experience to their areas of responsibility. Skillful leaders surrender control; they step back and ensure others also share in effective leadership. Finally, great leaders reflect on, and learn from, their personal and leadership experiences (Conchie, 2008).

As you read further, think of the leadership roles that you are involved in. You may be the CEO of an organization, a helper, a leader, a teacher, your child's soccer coach, a parent, or you may be in multiple leadership roles. Consider how you approach and fulfill this role.

Goleman and his colleagues (2002) noted:

> There are many leaders, not just one... leadership resides not

solely in the individual at the top, but in every person at every level who, in one way or another acts as a leader (p. xi).

Stephen Covey, the author of the *7 Habits of Highly Effective People*, states "at its most elemental and practical level, leadership is communicating to people their worth and potential so clearly that they come to see it in themselves" (Covey, 1990, p.98).

If there are areas of your leadership that you would like to enhance, the tools in this book will assist you to lead not only by position but with true passion and effectiveness.

## Shifting Your Leadership Style

As you reflect on your leadership style and experiences and consider making changes, it is important to learn first of all what exactly needs to change, and why it is necessary. Change is never easy, therefore, if you are unsure at this time why you need to shift your leadership style, now is the time for some reflection.

Perhaps you believe that how you are currently leading others is effective. Often when we behave in a certain way for a long time, our actions become habitual and it is difficult to see, with an unbiased eye, what behaviours might need altering.

If you are not clear on what is missing in your role as a leader, and how a change will benefit you and others, change will unfortunately be short-lived and ineffective. In this case it becomes easy to slip into habitual patterns of behaviour. Lasting change, on the other hand, requires contemplation, commitment, and action.

As you proceed, there are questions for you to consider. Reflect using a curious (not critical) eye to determine why you do what you do. Consider also how you can become a better leader and design a more supportive team/work environment. In order to learn about yourself and both what is working and what is not, it is often helpful to enlist the opinions of others, by asking for their perspectives on the situation.

As you begin to see areas in need of growth within yourself and your organization allow yourself to be with this knowledge in an accepting manner. This is the essence of mindfulness; being able to notice what is happening internally for you, in a non-judgmental manner. When practicing mindfulness, you begin to notice if you focus on problem solving, or worrying about the past or future. There is no need to fix, change or modify any of the observations you have had; with curious enquiry, continue to bring awareness to your own inner response.

The practice of mindfulness assists you to become aware of your thought patterns so that regardless of what is happening, you become aware of your own inner response, prior to responding. With mindfulness you notice if you become rigid and want to make changes immediately, or if you are able to be with your experiences just as they are, knowing that change will come as awareness increases. The best way to relax and gain clarity is to take five to ten deep breaths. As you breathe deeply and intentionally your body and internal responses automatically slow down and relax.

As you observe areas in yourself and in your environment that would benefit from change, practice noticing your inner reactions. You will find that as you become more cognizant of your internal responses, you will be more thoughtful and intentional in your actions.

Sometimes others may not be ready for change as quickly as you are, so allow yourself and this process to unfold in a gentle manner. As people observe changes in you, they too will change. It takes a great deal of effort to change, so ensure you are patient with yourself. Hold any patterns you observe with a light touch and make sure that you give yourself positive affirmations such as " I am doing my best" or "I am becoming more and more aware each day."

I once led an exercise on mindfulness with a group of health care practitioners. I asked them to focus on a person, place or thing that invokes a strong positive emotion for them and to notice where this feeling resides in their bodies. When I wrapped up this exercise, I asked the participants what they noticed about their experience. A few people reported that they felt that this exercise gave them hope for humanity and assisted them to feel more connected to themselves and to others. One woman, however, stood up and stated that her experience was not pleasant at all, because all she could think about was her dog defecating. This brought a lot of laughter from the group. I got the sense that she somehow thought she got it wrong, because her experience was not "nice and light." She had a thought and started to judge that thought.

Often times, we have experiences that we label as good, bad, or indifferent. It is important that we do not label our thoughts in this manner, but rather, be curious and laugh about our experiences and thoughts. Our minds take us in so many different directions, and if we grasp onto one thought in particular and question why it appears, we are not practicing mindfulness, we are practicing judgment.

As you engage in mindfulness practice, note with curiosity where your mind takes you, and let go of any criticism about what appears. Practicing in this manner allows deep acceptance of yourself and others.

Lead others with intention, wisdom, love and patience

Photo by S. March

# Family, Attachment & Core Beliefs

In order to gain insight as a leader we need to see how past experiences, current circumstances and future vision influence us. Dr. Daniel Siegel, a leading researcher in mindfulness and brain development, states that "our attachment style influences how we relate to others, how much breathing space we need in relationships, and how easily we can pick up on the mental state of another person" (Siegel 1999, p.89). It is important to explore our own early experiences because it impacts our leadership style in a number of areas including, but not limited to, how you receive support and encouragement, how you deal with challenges, how you give and receive feedback, how comfortable you are with emotional expression, and how you connect and disconnect from others.

Responses are shaped by early experiences and are often automatic, meaning, at a level that is rooted in the subconscious. If you have never considered why you do what you do, and the influence of your early experiences on your leadership style, you are not alone; quite often the influence of a person's family of origin has been given little or no attention (Munson, 1996, as cited in Caspi, 2002).

In early life, attachment relationships motivate infants to seek closeness to caregivers for support and nurture. How a person was nurtured, validated and supported will influence whether they become people who are more "hands off" or more "hands on" in relationships. Consequently, this impacts whether they prefer breathing space or closeness in relationships. If you were left on your own as a young person to explore the world, it may be that you have a desire or need for closeness, or you may have adapted to this, and are comfortable with distance. If you had a caregiver who was over-protective, you may have a desire for space or this may have created a need in you for closeness. We all adapt depending on what it is that helps us in being regulated and calm. Thus, because a caregiver was distant or over-protective does not mean we have developed a style of unavailability. Rather, it means that we have adapted to being sensitive to space and distance in all of our relationships. There is no pre-conceived response or equation to finding one's style, but when things become difficult your response is often driven by your primary style in relationships. Do you tend to isolate? Do you tend to seek out others? Understanding your response pattern during times of stress will assist you in gaining insight into your style of attachment. (If you are curious and would like to explore this subject in more depth, some psychologists are qualified to administer the Adult Attachment Interview (AAI)). While some leaders will be very "hands off", which may work well for those employees who enjoy and need autonomy, others may need more connection; they may feel unsupported or abandoned by such a leadership style. It is therefore important to be aware of one's own style and to learn what others need in a relationship in order to feel supported.

By knowing your style and understanding the style of those closest to you, you are better able to understand, relate to, and offer support to your colleagues and employees. Through awareness building, coaching, the support of friends or through psychotherapy, a person can grow their skills and become more relationally aware (Siegel, 1999). As your connection with others deepens, staff retention, happiness, productivity, and positivity will be enhanced by the improved relational style of leadership.

Following you will find some questions related to the influence of your first family. As you explore these, do so with curiosity. The people who raised you did the best job they could, and it is important to remember that their style of interacting was influenced by their parents and so forth. When I use the term "first family" I am referring to the family that raised you from the time you were young, or, the family that parented you until you reached age five.

## Questions for Self Reflection: Relating to My First Family

As you read these questions, know that there is nothing you need to do, fix, or change about yourself. It is awareness alone that assists us to grow and learn.

» How do you respond and what goes through your mind when others need comforting?

» How do you support others with an experience that is unfamiliar to them?

» How was expression of feelings and emotions encouraged or discouraged in your first family?

» What were the communication patterns /styles in your first family?

» Did you take on a specific role in your family (protector/caregiver)?

» How was insecurity dealt with?

» Are you more "hands off" or more "hands on" in relationships; do you prefer breathing space or closeness in relationships?

» How were limits set?

» Was there violence or abuse in your first family? If so, how do you respond to conflict now?

» How was tragedy dealt with?

» How did your first family express or show appreciation?

» What new insights do you have about how your first family impacts your leadership style?

» What strengths have you taken from your family that assists you as a leader?

» What areas do you need to grow, given your early family experiences?

# Mindfulness & Leadership

Mindfulness is defined in many distinct ways by countless experts. Although often associated with Buddhist practices, mindfulness can also be used in a secular manner to assist us with "refining our capacities for paying attention, for sustained awareness, and emergent insight" (Segal et al., 2002, p.viii).

Mindfulness takes us from being on automatic pilot to being increasingly in tune with ourselves and with others. Particularly in times of change, cultivating self-awareness through the practice of mindfulness assists leaders in releasing negative beliefs, judgments, and fears. "It also improves the leader's capacity to regulate emotions, combat emotional dysfunction, improve patterns of thinking, and reduce negative mindsets" (Siegel, 2007, p.6).

As you increase your mindfulness you will discover that you can deal with challenges and difficult situations in a powerful and effective manner. You will remain calm when others are stressed, you will experience a positive, balanced and happy state of mind and you will take responsibility for your actions and reactions. With increased awareness you will become more in tune with yourself and better able to respond to others.

It is important for you to notice what you are experiencing inwardly. Throughout the exercises in this book, and throughout your life, notice sensations, images, feelings and thoughts, and how they come and go from conscious thought (Siegel, 2007).

By becoming increasingly in tune with your internal responses, you will become a more mindful and present leader, and you will also learn how to slow things down and increase the space between thought and reaction. This ability to pause between thought and response is needed in leadership and in all areas of life. In *The 8th Habit*, Stephen Covey (2008) suggests that this space is determined by our genetic or biological inheritance, by upbringing and by our present circumstances. I believe that although this is true, that the space between thought and action can also be increased through mindfulness based practices. Becoming mindful will assist you to connect with your inner compass and consequently make sound, thoughtful decisions. As stated earlier, as you learn to become less reactive and more contemplative, you are able to reduce your fear and worry, be accepting, compassionate, calm and non-judgmental. As mentioned previously, the quickest and easiest way to nurture mindfulness is to focus on your breath. Slow down, relax, and breathe. As you integrate mindfulness into your life and work, you will realize amazing benefits.

## Profiling Progressive Organizations

Mindfulness is becoming increasingly sought after by organizations around the world. Although mindfulness based programs are commonly used to reduce stress, few programs have been developed to cultivate leadership, innovation and productivity in today's organizations.

One such program has been pioneered by Janice Marturano and Saki Santorelli. Ms. Marturano is the Vice President, Public Responsibility and Deputy General Counsel at General Mills, Inc. and Dr. Santorelli is the Executive Director at the University of Massachusetts' Center for Mindfulness in Medicine, Healthcare and Society. Ms. Marturano, a mindfulness teacher and a corporate officer for more than a decade and Dr. Santorelli, a world renowned teacher of mindfulness, partnered to develop a business-focused curriculum of intensive mindfulness training. The program entitled *Cultivating Leadership Presence through Mindfulness©* was originally offered to a small pilot group of General Mills officers and directors. The program quickly gained popularity with the organization and three years later more than 150 senior leaders at General Mills have participated in multi-day leadership programs.

Due to its huge success, the program has expanded beyond General Mills to include top leaders from more than 15 major organizations such as Cargill, Mayo Clinic, Ameriprise Financial and Medtronic.

Ms. Marturano reported that, "It is one of the most challenging and exciting times to be a leader and it is becoming increasingly apparent that we need to bring all of our capabilities to the present to lead effectively. This includes cultivating the mind's innate ability to be mindful; focused, open to what is in the present, and more able to see and develop strategic and innovative initiatives based on unbiased awareness. In the midst of all the pressures to 'check the box', now more than ever we need to lead by thinking outside the box."

The Center for Mindfulness currently offers a number of corporate programs including *Cultivating Leadership Presence through Mindfulness©* and *Catching Lightning: Mindfulness and Innovation©*. The Center also offers a seven week course entitled *Mindfulness in the Workplace©* which is an on-site course offered to employees at all levels. The courses can be tailored to meet specific business needs.

In a survey conducted with leaders who had attended one of the ten mindful leadership sessions taught by Ms. Marturano and Dr. Santorelli; 93% of attendees reported that the program had a positive impact on their ability to take time to reflect, creating space for discovery and innovation. Furthermore, 89% of respondents reported that the program enhanced their ability to listen to themselves and to others. And nearly 70% of attendees reported that the program made a positive difference in their ability to think strategically.

Nursing staff in the rural community of Canmore, Alberta, Canada have also been utilizing mindfulness-based training. Ms. Shellian, the manager with Alberta Health Services responsible for the implementation of this program, stated that as a result of participating in this program, staff members reported feeling more positive and found they were better able to handle the difficulties of their jobs in a more optimistic manner. In addition, they reported feeling better able to handle the stresses of the job.

Mindfulness-based programs assist leaders in bringing greater compassion to others and in dealing with world problems in a manner that is clear and insightful. As leaders learn about this innate ability to be mindful, they are better able to assist others to learn and grow. Although training the mind and practicing awareness-raising skills requires dedication and commitment, the results are rewarding as leaders transform their environments into places of increased compassion, innovation and productivity.

Free your dreams to soar!

Photo by H. March

# Vision & Values

It is through our values and vision that we determine what is important to us and how we will shape our lives. Vision is seeing a future state with the mind's eye. Vision is applied imagination and occurs first of all in the mind through a process of considering desires, dreams, hopes, goals and plans. Vision is then made manifest through actions and plans (Covey, 2004). Values are those beliefs that shape who we are. As you consider your vision and your core values and beliefs, think about the values you hold as highly important; values that define "who you are."

I have found in my own life that when I have a very clear vision things happen effortlessly. I decided approximately one year before I published this book that this is what I planned to do. Within three months of my intended date for publication, I met my editor while snowshoeing, I met my designer through a business acquaintance and I met the woman who designed the book cover for me at a dinner party. I had many friends submit photographs: everyone I met seemed to bend over backwards to assist me. If you are unsure about why things might not be happening in your life, check in with your vision and see what you are creating and inviting into your world. If you feel that your life is not in line with what you want to create, spend some time and consider what might be stopping or blocking you.

In *Leadership and the New Science*, Margaret Wheatley (2007) writes that both organizations and the individuals within them need a clear sense of their values, traditions, history, dreams, experiences, competencies, and culture. Clear vision and values are necessary for fulfillment, both individually and organizationally.

We all have different values, and we need to remember that when it appears someone is disrespecting our values it is simply this: they hold a different value than ours. If you feel like someone is dishonoring your values, it is likely done unconsciously and with no intention to cause harm. Instead, recognize that two different value systems are coming together. It is very important not to label others as wrong in their values as they are just as important to them as yours are to you. You need to hold on to your values but recognize that if you are triggered by what you perceive as disrespect you need to let it go, knowing that you don't need to be right. Letting go of the need to be right will bring you peace. In addition, honoring the uniqueness of each other's values will assist you in being more tolerant, kind, compassionate and relational.

Today's leader needs to be clear in his or her own values and beliefs, vision, and in tune with everything and everyone around him or her. Like a lighthouse that is solid and strong, they must guide and protect, look forward and all around, and assist others to achieve their potential.

On the next page there is a list of values. Note that there are a lot of values not on this list, so please ensure you add your own if a value that is important to you is not listed.

» Circle your top five values.

» Which of these is your top value?

» Remember a high point in your life. What was happening then?

» Name the value that was being honored:

_____

» Think of something you cannot give up in your life (beyond the obvious examples of food and shelter).

» What is necessary for you to have in your life?

» Name the value you cannot live without:

_____

» What is it that you really want, that you don't have?

» How are you honoring that value on a scale of 1 to 10 (with 1 being poor and 10 being great)?

» Imagine one year from now: how do you want things to be?

» What new insights do you have about your values and beliefs?

» Is there a belief or behaviour you need to release?

» Is there a belief or behaviour you need to embrace?

## Values

| | | |
|---|---|---|
| Abundance | Freedom | Honesty |
| Hope | Humility | Independence |
| Joy | Justice | Service |
| Achievement | Ambition | Challenge |
| Charity | Dignity | Enjoyment |
| Equality | Excellence | Security |
| Faith | Family | Patience |
| Kindness | Leadership | Integrity |
| Love | Loyalty | Obedience |
| Power | Recognition | Relationships |
| Respect | Safety | Trust |
| Wealth | Adventure | Spontaneity |

# Tuning Into Self

As you become clear in your values and vision, you will have a better idea about the things that are important to you. Becoming more in tune with ourselves can create fundamental shifts in thought and behaviour.

As you explore the following sections, notice your own reactions and responses and proceed in a mindful and conscious manner. Bring awareness to yourself, your responses and your thoughts and feelings. You need to understand your responses: do you respond with grace, lightness and humor, not taking yourself or the world too seriously, or do you grasp and resist?

Even if you are unsure as to how you are going to make something happen, the power of declaring an intention out loud and in writing holds a lot of power. Contemplate what it is that you are committed to as a leader. The power of the imagination is very strong indeed; nurture it in yourself and in others.

Think about your own current vision and plans for your role as a leader.

- » Spend some time and outline your dreams, hopes, goals and plans for yourself.
- » What are the things that bring you great joy as you lead others?
- » How often do you experience or practice those things?
- » What beliefs do you hold about how leaders should act, react, and inspire others?
- » Are these views serving you and others, or, are they impeding growth?
- » Do you trust the people you lead, and are you able to surrender control?
- » Are you able to stay calm and grounded in times where others are stressed, frustrated or angry?
- » How do you stay calm and grounded?

Think about someone you consider a great leader and how they demonstrate their leadership abilities:

- » What does this person have to teach you?
- » What action step can you take towards becoming the leader you desire to be?
- » How will you apply what you have learned?
- » What new behavioural changes are required?

# Tuning Into Others

In order to tune into others, you need to be able to offer support, be a teacher, and be an effective communicator. Think about how you currently learn about yourself as a leader. Do you use 360 degree feedback tools and open dialogue, or do you measure your success in another way? Do you avoid feedback altogether, fearing what people might say?

Although it might be somewhat unnerving asking people what they think of you, what they appreciate about you, and where they feel you need to improve, it is by far the most revealing way of learning about yourself and your blind spots.

Where clear sight is blocked, and if someone sees something about you that you cannot accept, remember that their insight is a gift to you which may prove invaluable. We must try not to take feedback as criticism but as insight we can incorporate into our lives.

## Self Reflection Exercise: Start Asking Around

Ask three people if they would be candid with you regarding your strengths and weaknesses. These people need to know there will not be any repercussions for being honest. Tell them what you are attempting to do, why it is important to you, and how they can help you achieve your goal. People may be auditory or visual learners so be considerate that they may need time to contemplate before responding. They may also prefer to have the questions in a written format.

As you prepare to ask your colleagues or employees how they experience you as a leader, first of all take some time and do a self-assessment. Consider whether you think that others perceive you as being available and approachable. Also, do you feel like you know what is important and meaningful to the people you lead? Do you know what others need from you? Do you know how much or little support the people you lead require? Do people leave your organization and you are left not knowing why?

Spend some time and explore the questions on the next page and reflect on how you think other people will respond. If you find that when you ask these questions that your own perceptions are consistent with the responses that you get, then this will demonstrate that you are in tune with how others experience you. Regardless of what you learn, look at how you can use this information to become a more mindful leader.

## Questions to Ask:

» Do you think I am in touch with how you learn best and how you like to receive feedback? If not, tell me about yourself and how I can better support you?

» What are my strengths as a leader?

» What are the areas I need to grow in?

» On a scale of 1-10, How often do I give compliments and acknowledgment (with 1 being poor and 10 being great)?

» Do I follow through on commitments in a timely manner? If this has not happened, what do you need from me?

» Do you respond quickly or do you need time to contemplate a question or issue?

» Do you like to have things conveyed verbally or in writing?

» If there is a problem or a miscommunication, how do you prefer it to be handled?

» If you are frustrated with me, do you find that I am approachable and you can bring your concerns to me?

» Do you trust that I will not become defensive?

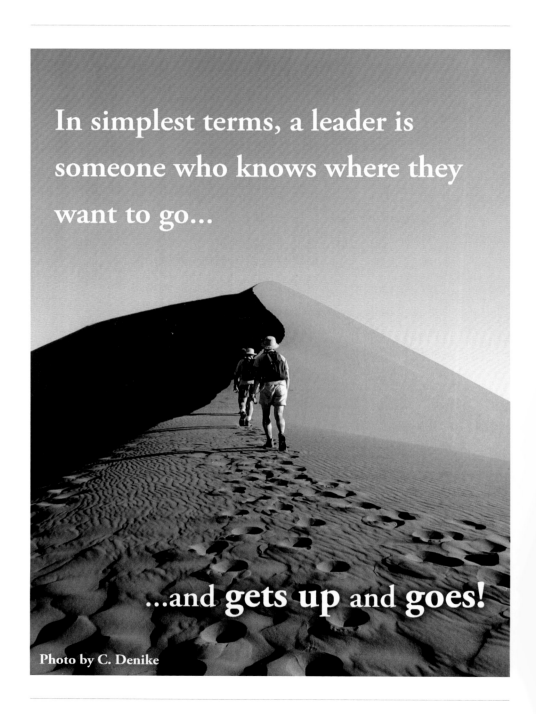

In simplest terms, a leader is someone who knows where they want to go...

...and **gets up** and **goes!**

Photo by C. Denike

# Creating Awareness Through Mind & Body

Awareness can be developed by looking at processes and situations concretely and cognitively, or by tuning into your intuition and the sensations and feelings in your body.

If you find that you have a habit of over-thinking and that you sometimes ruminate on problems and try to figure things out in your head, it is suggested that you focus more strongly on the body-based interventions in this book. It has been shown that ruminating gives us less access to creativity and resources and makes us less in tune with ourselves and others (Segal, 2002). If you know you have a tendency or preference for one mode over another, ensure that you try the ones that are more uncomfortable for you in order to learn something new.

Often times when we are having a difficult time we can over-focus on thinking and focus less on what is going on in our bodies. It is the mind's job to keep you safe and secure, to focus on your survival. Fear, old habits, and patterns keep you doing the same things, even when the results are unsatisfying. Body based interventions with a mindfulness component can assist people who are "thinkers" to become more in tune with their bodies and to make lasting changes. Body based interventions can be facilitated through the practice of meditation, yoga, and movement, or by bringing awareness to sensations and feelings in your body.

In my own work as a yoga instructor, I experienced first-hand the benefit of bringing yoga and mindfulness to others. For a period of approximately six months, I facilitated yoga classes for youths and adults at an in-patient hospital psychiatric unit. The classes integrated yoga, visualization and mindfulness. I observed that people experienced a decrease in intensity of emotional affect and disturbing thoughts after participating in the classes.

Many participants reported that the class helped them to be more relaxed, to release negative thoughts and to be more peaceful. In one particular class, I taught a man with a patch over one eye and a young girl covered in cuts from self harming. I pondered, that since our outer appearances either invite connection or invite distance, and our inner worlds are shaped by the reactions of others, how can we bring greater compassion to others and help them to see their self worth? Throughout the class, these two people in particular were willing to try something new and to be adventurous. They trusted me when I told them they would feel better after yoga. At one point in the class, the gentlemen with the eye patch told me that if I touched him he would bite me. I told him that I would not touch him unless it was okay with him, and that he better not bite me! By doing so I hoped to communicate my acceptance of his wishes, and that it was a worthy request not to be touched. I shared with him the intention of touch was to assist him to do the postures (which are called Asanas in yoga) in a safe manner. He happily agreed... and I didn't get bitten! After this class I further thought about how at our core, we all want the same things: to be accepted, loved and appreciated. We set up many barriers to create distance from others and we have learned to protect ourselves from rejection in whatever way necessary. Sometimes we see people as unsafe because our past experiences have shielded us from seeing the kindness and good intentions of others.

Canadian Counsellor and Yoga Therapist, Robin Campbell, states that through reflective processing using mindfulness based therapies, the gains made by bringing conscious awareness to feelings and sensations in your body are far superior to cognitive reflection alone. In addition, he believes that when you assist someone to be able to get in touch with their own feelings, they experience significant shifts in their lives and in their way of being.

Consider for yourself how you invite relationships and how you guard yourself. It is through mindfulness that you will be able to slow down, listen to yourself, learn about your own patterns, and choose which to keep and which to let go.

## Self Reflection Exercise: Using Cognitive Processes

One way of becoming more mindful is through cognitive processes aimed at self-reflection. Here are the steps to take:

### Part A: Mindfully Observing Your Thoughts

» Think of something or someone that is meaningful to you, or think of something specific that is bothering you.

» Observe your mind

» What thoughts are you having?

» Write down three or four sentences describing your thoughts.

» Practicing mindfulness, and without labeling your thoughts as good or bad, notice where they tend to be directed.

» Notice your observation of your thoughts- Are you condemning them, or approaching them with interest and curiosity?

» Do your thoughts tend to be optimistic or focused on worry, concerns or problems?

» Do this practice regularly in order to become in tune with your thoughts.

## Self Reflection Exercise: Using Cognitive Processes

### Part B: Taking Action

» Begin by thinking about a challenging situation you are currently facing

» Practice non-judgmental acceptance of your thoughts.

» Be solution oriented-If this situation could be improved by 10% what would be different?

» If a miracle occurred and this difficulty was solved, how would you know that a miracle occurred?

» Write down what would be different.

» What positive difference will this make for you?

» Be observant and notice when small bits of the miracle show up in your life.

## Self Reflection Exercise: Increasing Body Awareness

Spend a minute thinking of one area where you have a specific frustration with an issue, person, or situation. If you find that you are resistant to doing this, it could be a sign that there is something for you to learn. It is being shown through resistance and fear, but trust you can handle whatever messages you receive.

» Begin by observing what is happening in your body, and what feelings you are experiencing as you think about this concern.

» This may be challenging to identify, but take a minute and close your eyes and scan your body slowly, from your feet to the top of your head.

» Typically, when we are in a situation that causes us stress or frustration, we will become aware of a bodily sensation that accompanies it.

» As you scan your body—what do you notice?

» All you need to do is breathe.

» Take five deep cleansing breaths directed specifically into the area where you notice the feeling in your body.

» Stay with this feeling and notice it in more detail. Imagine this feeling has a shape, color, and size.

» See if it moves or wants to move.

» Continue to take five more deep breaths.

» Learn what message this feeling in your body has for you. It is there for a reason. Learn the wisdom in it.

» Bring awareness to yourself, your responses, your thoughts and feelings; this in itself can create fundamental shifts.

» The question to remember to ask is "What is this like right now"?

» What am I aware of right now?

» What do I want to remember from right now?

» What action step do I need to take moving forward?

If you have read through this exercise and chose not to do it, consider if there are thoughts in your mind such as "I don't have the time; this is a waste of time." Don't label the message wrong, instead, be aware of it.

Even when the path seems to

take you uphill

find time
to play!

Photo by A. Bennett

# Emotional Intelligence & Leadership

Conscious mindful leaders live their lives in a compassionate and loving manner. They consider how their actions impact others and act with wisdom. They are approachable, understanding and thoughtful. They typically have a high degree of what is called Emotional Intelligence.

Emotional Intelligence, studied extensively by Daniel Goleman, assists you to be in touch with your own feelings and emotions and to be in tune with others. It is comprised of a number of different skills including assertiveness, optimism, flexibility, problem-solving, self-awareness, social sensitivity, empathy and an ability to communicate successfully with others. Your emotional quotient (EQ) is vital as emotional competence accounts for the majority of success in the highest levels of leadership (Goleman, 1995).

Do you find that you are in tune with the needs of others and that you are able to notice when people are struggling, or do people tell you that you are not aware of conflicts or difficult situations until they amplify to the point of sirens and fireworks? In addition, do you know how to respond when someone else is upset or frustrated?

One of the primary components of emotional intelligence is empathy. Empathy requires engaging with interest, responsiveness, and attunement to others. Responding to an employee's emotional state may be challenging, but it is a very important part of leadership.

By showing interest in the emotional wellbeing of others you are letting them know you care and are there for them. This sort of relationship fosters employee loyalty. Gilbreath & Benson (2004) found that if employees rated their supervisor's behaviour above average, the probability was 63% that their psychological well-being score would also be above average. Numerous researchers have identified that leaders or supervisors often do not actively attend to employee's emotional experiences. As you become clear about your own comfort level with emotional expression, you will better be able to tolerate emotions that may have once been uncomfortable for you. As you become more empathetic, others will report feeling understood by you and in turn, be more productive and positive. Leaders with highly developed EQ are in tune with what is going on around them.

In these uncertain economic times, it is especially important for leaders to be supportive and understanding. Bernhut (2002) summarizes Goleman, Boyatzis & McKee (2002) by stating that:

> In a climate of uncertainty, primal leadership becomes more important than ever, because people need a leader who lends an air of certainty, or at least conviction, a sense of "this is where we're heading these days," at a time when fears and anxieties can overtake them. All of this is particularly important because of the relationship—which is neurologically based—between emotions and attention and cognition. That is, the ability to get

work done depends on our emotions not being out of control. A leader has to speak to those often-unstated fears along the way in order to help people keep them under control.

You will find that as you become more in tune with what is going on in your environment, the more likely it is that you will notice cues that something is amiss early on. As a result you can be preventative in your approach and able to support others more effectively. If you find that you tend not to notice subtle interpersonal cues, this is something you will need to enhance in order to become an effective and responsive leader. When others feel that you understand them, they are more likely to be loyal, happy, and content.

## Self Reflection Exercise: How's Your EQ?

Emotional Intelligence is created and nurtured through the process of increasing self awareness and through mindfulness.

By reflecting on the following questions, you will gain some insight regarding areas that are difficult for you and those that seem easier. By noticing uncomfortable responses or sensations in your body you can learn to explore them with a curious mind. Enhancing your EQ will assist you in becoming more relational, aware, and connected with other people.

» How much attention do you pay to your feelings and intuition?
» Are you able to tolerate uncomfortable feelings in yourself?
» Are you most often grounded and centered or do you often feel anxious or worried?
» When there is conflict are you able to lean into it and explore what wants to happen or do you tend to avoid it?
» Are you able to inspire others by appealing to their values and aspirations?
» Are you able to notice and ask about sadness, frustration or anger in others?

## Self Reflection Exercise: Developing Your EQ

Often when we are faced with a challenging situation we lose our ability to tap into our wisdom and to think creatively. One way to find a solution that comes from a place of wisdom is to ask the question "What would love do?" You don't need to tell anyone you are asking yourself this question; this is purely for yourself. It may seem too nebulous, but be willing to push this a bit and see what comes to you.

In difficult times and challenging circumstances, you find wisdom in asking the "What would love do" question. Love will look differently depending on the circumstances you encounter. Love is an attitude you embody when you are acting from a place of deep respect for self and others. Love does not mean giving in to someone; love may be saying "No" or it may be saying "Yes".

Among others, I have asked pilots, electricians, and business people this question and I am typically met by a blank stare. But, after a few minutes a response comes from a place of wisdom and deep knowing. Trust this, and give it a try.

So, in the midst of your challenge, what would love do?

When your

entire world seems

**upside down**

you can either fight it or

choose

**another**

**perspective**

that is

**playful and curious**

Photo by E. Thompson

# Mindful Communication

Communication is fundamental to all we do. At work, we make decisions, plan and direct our daily activities using communication. Both our professional and personal success depends largely on our ability to build and sustain meaningful relationships with people. Clear, open and effective communication is one of the most valuable skills we can possess.

As you reflect on those behaviours you engage in that support positive communication and those that inhibit it, you will be better equipped to choose behaviours and responses that are helpful. Fundamentally, at our core we all want three things: to be seen and appreciated for who we are; to have our opinions and views heard by others; and to make a difference in the world. It is our responsibility to ensure that we are using the skills of communication including; listening, responding, initiating, and questioning capably, so that we are supporting others to the best of our abilities.

Listening is a fundamental skill and component of mindful communication. Think of a time when you really focused on listening to another person in order to understand them and when someone really listened to you. Bring to your communication a deep honoring of the other person for who they are. When you respond to another person, ensure they have your complete attention and that you are not multitasking or distracted. If you are distracted, be honest and set up another time to meet.

When asking questions, it is important to ask purposeful questions as a way of learning more and to approach situations from a stance of curiosity. When questions are posed in a manner that is curious, the questions become less directive, punitive and confrontational and more collaborative. To put it simply, talk to people with and from your heart. This will bring genius, honesty, authenticity, and will assist the other person in feeling valued and appreciated. If you are unsure how to do this, consider an instance where you felt deeply appreciated by someone else. Bring this feeling into your communications.

Here is a simple acronym that is useful and easy to remember. As you use it, you will REAP the benefits!

**R** emain Calm
**E** xpress Feelings
**A** ssess what is going on for me
**P** ractice Patience

As leaders and managers relate to others in a conscious, mindful manner, organizations and individual employees thrive and experience positive attitudes and productivity in the workplace and in our world.

# Appreciation & Acknowledgement

Leaders of organizations are responsible to model interactions that facilitate kindness and thoughtfulness at work, encourage employees to deal with conflict in an open and constructive manner, and to ensure the work environment is supportive. Research indicates that the most positive and productive environments are those where people are given four positive statements to every one negative/corrective statement.

According to a survey of a number of the Fortune 500 companies, 94.4% of the people who report the highest morale at work agree that their managers are effective at positive recognition. Additionally, according to an Ipsos Reid poll taken in the United States, there is a near unanimous agreement: 95% of people polled stated they feel "really good when others thank me for something I have done or accomplished."

Nearly all respondents (94%) stated a belief that "more than anything else, getting a genuine thank you from someone is the best kind of reward that you can get." In fact, when asked about the most meaningful reward they have ever received, the most common unprompted answer is a "sincere thank you." (Ipsos Reid, 2008b).

It is important to recognize whether you have a tendency to give or withhold compliments. Check back to your first family experiences.

We all have a habitual style, and as we become more conscious of this tendency, we can look and see if this is working for us and giving us the results we desire or not. When giving compliments to others, remember that it is important to be specific, as people need to know what they are being appreciated for. Reflect on where you hold back compliments or acknowledgment.

Every so often my friend and former business partner, Chris, writes me an email that says, "I just wanted to tell you, you rock!" I love it when I get these emails from him. Knowing I have a tendency to be hard on myself, it reminds me to not only accept appreciation from others, but to be more kind and appreciative to myself. I also am more likely to extend appreciation when experiencing its usefulness in my life.

There are many wonderful visionaries who suggest that we should strip away the ego's need for validation and appreciation to get to the core of who we are. I agree that we need to not rely on the words of others to give us self worth. However, there is a pure value in appreciating and honoring others and sharing the difference that they make for us in the world.

Strengths can serve as a foundation on which to build. Do your best not to offer negative feedback between positive compliments. Let each stand on its own and trust that the employee is able to handle it. Complimenting can help to boost another's confidence and motivation. Latting (1992) found that the desire to perform well is often enhanced through extrinsic rewards such as supervisor praise.

Consider how you approach appreciation. If you consistently get feedback that this is an area that needs improvement, listen and respond accordingly.

People love to laugh, have fun and to be appreciated. Connection between people is missing in many work environments, so I always enjoy facilitating workshops that bring fun, connection, humor and insight at the same time. I recently used an activity with a group of administrative assistants to assist them to think creatively and have fun. When facilitating this activity, I bring my tickle trunk of props and have everyone take one. These props vary from dinosaurs (from my previous work as a play therapist) to paint brushes and party hats. I then have people in groups design a story that has a beginning, middle and end using their props. The story must have some climax, drama and resolution. This is a very fun way to get people laughing and having fun. After the activity, we talked about how this applies to mindfulness. One woman shared that we so often use an item for the purpose we are told that it is for; that we forget or don't think it could be used in other ways. I had brought a money belt for traveling and one woman had pretended she was a horse, and had tied the money belt around her neck as if it was a feed trough—very creative indeed! We relate to ourselves and our thoughts in a similar manner. Without mindfulness, we get ingrained in patterns of behaving and thinking that are limiting. With increased mindfulness, we gain clarity and have more freedom with our thoughts and actions.

## Self Reflection Exercise: Extending Appreciation

» How do you currently show appreciation to others?

» Think of a time when someone verbally appreciated you. What did they say and how did this impact you?

» Recall when someone complimented you. How did this feel? If it felt strange, know that this does not make it wrong, just different from what you are used to.

» Identify one person with whom you work closely. Name their top three strengths

» Name of person _____

1.

2.

3.

Now, go and tell that person what you wrote about them.

# Mindfulness Saboteurs

A saboteur is a feature designed by the psyche to keep a person living in the status quo; the place of safety and comfort. A mindfulness saboteur wreaks havoc on your peace of mind and causes stress, upset and frustration. It is your job to notice when this occurs and put the saboteur in its place.

Even though the saboteurs occur as challenges, they provide us with an opportunity to process and practice mindfulness. After discussing each of these saboteurs, strategies will then be suggested on how to manage them.

## Saboteur 1: Negative Mindsets

As a leader, it is important to investigate how you approach learning. Your mindset and perspective impact how you live your life and whether you passively accept events or whether you are an active creator of your life. How you live your life moment to moment is a choice, and how you arrive at work is a result of that choice.

If you take pause, you will notice that your mental chatter begins from the moment you awake until the moment you fall asleep. By slowing things down and becoming more reflective, you will become increasingly aware of your unconscious habits and tendencies and you will be able to relate to others with increased awareness, and, as a result of this practice, become a stronger and more effective leader.

Consider how you currently approach situations in your life. Are you an optimist or a pessimist? Do you believe you live in a world of abundance or in one where there is not quite enough to go around? Do you approach life as a competitor or as a collaborator? Notice how your perspective pervades every aspect of your life, and consider, if you are in a state of fear or worry, what might be possible if you took on a more empowering perspective.

Many people go through life believing that their negative emotions are a direct result of the experiences that they have and that they have no control over them. I would like to suggest that negative emotions are a direct result of our "beliefs" about our experiences. We often give too much attention to the emotions we feel, emotions that often result from frustration. When we respond, it is in reaction to our emotions. Is it your tendency to withdraw when upset or angry, or is it your tendency to act out? By recognizing your reaction, you can start to bring more awareness to common habits, including emotional reactivity, and make more effective choices.

Most often feelings of frustration and disappointment occur when we feel misunderstood, when we want to say something but were unable to, if we have an attachment to things going or being a certain way, or if we have an expectation that has not been met. In *How to be an Adult in Relationships*, David Richo (2002) writes that frustration may arise when one of the following situations occur:

» You feel that another person poses a threat.
» You believe that someone can provide you with something you need.
» You have a belief about someone and it obscures what he or she is really like.
» You feel attached to a particular outcome and get caught in the need to fix, persuade, advise, or change another person.
» You may also find that when things do not go your way, that you become judgmental or critical.

Notice which of these mindsets occurs most often for you and practice catching it before it amplifies into actions or reactions.

## Saboteur 2: Triggers

Before losing our cool, it is important to know the issues that cause us to become upset or frustrated before they affect the situation in a negative manner.

When challenging situations appear for us, the more aware we are that they may cause us to become triggered, the more skillful we can become in our responses.

The part of the brain responsible for planning and organizing is called the prefrontal cortex. This area usually helps with compassionate communication and empathy, and enables us to make rational, thoughtful, and flexible choices. When triggered, sub-cortical activation interferes with effective executive functioning, and thus, our ability to plan, problem solve, process, think creatively and be patient is diminished.

Some indications you have been triggered include being inflexible or rigid in your perspective, having anger flare ups, or being flooded by emotions including fear, confusion, sadness, or rage. In addition, you may feel frustration, shame, or any other strong emotion. It is important to slow things down and notice what happens in your body when you first become triggered. These physical responses are called warning signs. When you become aware of the warning signs arising for you, take a moment to evaluate the situation. If you find that you have a tendency to act out, speak out, yell out, and usually respond from a place of anger or frustration, it is more than likely your response will not be effective or helpful. Thoughts cause our feelings and behaviours, not external things like people, situations, and events. We can change the way we think and feel even if the situation does not change.

Anger occurs when we feel that we have been wronged, when we are unable to express our true feelings, or when we have an expectation that has not been met. Normally, when we think of someone or something that causes us frustration, anger occurs. It is normal and natural, and it is an opportunity to learn something about ourselves.

Many people are not in tune with their bodies and don't notice subtle sensations or feelings. Sometimes, when asked to focus on sensations in their bodies, people report that they do not feel anything. We all have a range of emotions, some are readily observable such as tears of sadness, but sometimes subtler emotions are more difficult to notice.

It may be necessary to sit still in order to be able to notice subtle body sensations. Sitting and being with your own feelings and sensations provides vital information. As you are still you will hear your own wisdom; this practice requires patience and perseverance.

## Self Reflection Exercise: What Triggers You?

As you investigate your response to being triggered, bring awareness to sensations, feelings and thoughts you are having. Often, recalling a frustrating situation will invoke the same physiological response that you had when the actual event occurred.

Identify a situation in your role as a leader that caused you frustration.

» What happened that upset you?

» What did you do?

» What did you say to yourself about the other person or situation?

» Which of the following occur when you are upset?

　　» You have a strong emotional reaction

　　» You may act impulsively

　　» You may not accurately perceive what is happening

　　» You may have sensations in your body that tell you something is not right

　　» You may be inflexible or rigid in your perspective

　　» You may blame someone else and see them as the source of the problem

　　» You will claim that the person really is the problem

Holding a rigid perspective and blaming others for difficulties often comes from feeling powerless and frustrated. Do not take action or deal with others when you are feeling triggered. Take some time for yourself to calm down and reflect on what is occurring for you internally. Notice your reactions, responses and feelings.

## Saboteur 3: Dealing with Difference

Another habit that wreaks havoc on our mental peace is non-acceptance. One of the primary reasons we have so much hatred and war in this world is because we assume those people that are different from us are wrong. Having asked executives and managers what their biggest challenges are, they most often reply that they find it difficult to deal with the person who wants to do things differently, or who is different.

Often the person with a viewpoint that is different from the majority gets labeled as bad, difficult, or problematic. This labeling process is amplified when the person who holds an opinion different from the norm is cynical, resigned or outspoken.

Why do we feel that those people who hold different opinions are wrong? I suggest that it is for three reasons: firstly, we have a desire to have things done our way or we have a rigid view of how things need to be done; secondly, we have an inflexible attitude towards difference; and thirdly, we are very strongly attached to our value system. It is important to notice our response when we have discomfort because someone is different or has different ideas.

Difference has more to teach us than consensus. It needs to be explored with curiosity and not reacted to, or defended against. It is important to see how, as a leader, you can embrace this difference. As you approach difficulties or challenges, ask yourself: what does this person need and what do I need? If there is something that you are struggling with, speak it before resentment builds up. Address the person and situation in a manner that is calm, fair, firm, and direct. Also, when speaking, consider how you can make the situation better for all parties involved. If you start from a position of helpfulness and kindness, the other person will feel your positive energy and be more open to dialogue and discussion. If you are struggling with this concept, read on to learn how to address these challenges. You could also consider gaining the support of a leadership coach to assist you in this growth process.

What are circumstances or situations that cause you the most frustration? I become frustrated when someone I am traveling with has a different idea about how early we need to be at the airport before departure. We have different ideas about time management and we have different stress thresholds. It is not that we, or the other person, are intentionally trying to be difficult, but rather, we have different ways of doing things. I would like to be at the airport in a timely manner, and alleviate any stress associated with a late arrival. My friend is happy to go with the flow and arrive minutes before the flight leaves. When there are situations that arise between individuals with conflicting styles, it is especially important that you discuss and plan prior to the event. It is during the event that stress is high, and our ability to problem solve is diminished. Pre-planning, discussion and compromise are three very important skills to use in any relationship. Be preventative so that both parties feel heard and when different values or ways of doing things arise, you can build on your strengths and open communication to get you through.

## Self Reflection Exercise: Inviting Difference

Now think about a situation where you experience a challenge because someone does things differently than you do.

» What are the three things that cause you the most frustration?

» How do you deal with this difference now?

» Do you feel upset or frustrated with someone when they hold a view that differs from yours?

» When this occurs, what behaviours do you engage in?

» What sorts of thoughts do you have?

» What happens in your body (feelings, sensations) when you have a rigid or limiting perspective?

» What can you do as a leader to encourage multiple perspectives and honor differences amongst team-members?

» How can you handle this challenge in a manner that is preventative?

Have the **vision** to **reach** beyond obstacles to achieve your goals

Photo by C. Harbin

# Dealing with Difficult Relationships/ Communication Breakdowns

We all experience difficult relationships and misunderstandings at times. Disconnections are normal in any relationship. What is important is how we respond to these breakdowns and challenges. If you find yourself feeling isolated and alone, know that you can take the time to reflect on what is going on before you respond. Consider that what might be happening is a trigger from childhood, or a response to feeling abandoned or smothered. Alternately, the challenge might be arising because as discussed earlier in the book, your values may be opposing someone else's values. Take the time to reflect on your internal landscape and listen to what it is teaching you about yourself.

Steps towards dealing with a challenge:

» Take a deep breath and relax.
» Go into the situation with a mind focused on repairing the relationship.
» Be aware of the other person's signals and your own needs.
» Focus on how to reconnect with the person (you will need to know something about what they need in times of conflict or challenge).
» Focus on being kind and compassionate to yourself.
» Set limits and state your own needs.
» If upset, come back to the other person after calming down.

» If you are in the midst of a heated discussion, rather than just leaving, let the other person know that you need a break and will return to the conversation.

» It is helpful to be preventative and to discuss with the other person how much time is needed to cool off in times of conflict. By having this discussion before any conflict occurs, it is much easier to call a time-out and take a break in the midst of turbulent times.

## Tools to Deal with the Saboteurs

As previously mentioned, the saboteur, a feature of the psyche that prevents growth and empowerment, can arise in many situations, including when you have a negative mind-set, when you are triggered, and when you are dealing with difference. In addition to the practices just suggested, there are some other ways that you can notice when a saboteur is active and try to ensure that it does not sabotage you.

To begin with, notice the following in order to observe how active your saboteur is in your daily life.

The saboteur can show up in our self-talk. If you notice that you are using words and phrases like, "I should, I have to, I ought to, I don't know, I cannot because I have to…" catch yourself and recognize that often-times these statements prevent growth.

The saboteur can also prevent us from accomplishing or achieving the things that we say are really important to us. One way to get yourself on track is by ensuring your goals are GREAT goals.

**G** entle
**R** ealistic
**E** xciting
**A** ttainable
**T** imely

Check in with yourself regarding something that you have been saying you would like to do, but have not yet done. You may have many reasons why you have not done the thing that you say you wish to do. However, it is likely that there is a saboteur in action. If you find that this is happening for you, use the GREAT strategy to get you back on track.

## Self Reflection Exercise: Managing the Saboteur

There are a number of mindfulness practices to assist you in dealing with the saboteur. The saboteur likes it when you aren't grounded, centered or skilled. In order to gain confidence and skill, try this practice in order to ground yourself.

### Grounding

» Step one: Notice sensations in your body.

» Step two: Label whatever feeling it is that comes up, "I am feeling frustrated."

» Step three: If your complaint is about somebody else, know that this person, just like you, struggles to be happy. Stop relating to this person and yourself as an object to be dealt with, something in your way, or something to help you; see their humanity and worth.

» Step four: If it is hard to let it go, do not be hard on yourself because this is also part of the human condition. Practice patience with yourself and with others. Give yourself and the other person space and time to calm down; do your own inner work then return to the situation.

# Leadership & Teams

There is a high likelihood that if you are reading this book, you work with or within a team. As you reflect on the previous sections, and how you lead, think now about the atmosphere in your environment. If someone were to come in off the street, would they have the sense that it is a sunny environment, or a cloudy environment? Have there been heavy rains or a tornado? Often dynamics in an environment impact all employees and customers and influences productivity, positivity and communication.

It appears that, for some Canadians, "a negative workplace culture might be getting in the way of productivity, with an Ipsos Reid poll revealing that one in three (31%) Canadian workers agree (8% strongly/23% somewhat) that it's difficult for them to 'concentrate fully on the task at hand' in their workplace because they're 'dragged down by a negative atmosphere at work' (Ipsos Reid, 2008a).

Rigidity in organizations and amongst its people occurs when there is a fear of change, or when the risk of change seems too great. Individuals behave in a manner that maintains the status quo which inadvertently prevents growth and creates conflict.

In teams where people feel included, there is an atmosphere of partnership and a sense that it is okay to ask questions and engage in communication with leaders. Furthermore, when people are verbally appreciated and acknowledged, more positive outcomes were noted than in environments where leaders were less relationally focused. Five good things that emerge from growth-fostering relationships are zest, empowerment for action, clarity, increased sense of worth, and the desire for more connection (Jean Baker Miller (1986) as cited in Downs, 2006).

Aside from the self-reflection skills noted earlier, to be a mindful leader you need to be able to:

» Stay Calm      » Be Inviting

» Be Fair      » Build Trust

» Be Firm

## The Challenge of Organizational Distress

It is helpful to recognize that challenging employees, who are often presented as "disturbers", may have important information to teach you about the needs of your organization. Premature "firing" can lead to a whole host of other challenges in your organization. For instance, if a vocal employee is fired for "rocking the boat" other employees may have a fear of speaking up. They might feel that by expressing an unpopular opinion they are at risk of losing their job. Often after a disturber is fired a new disturber will arise. It may be someone within the organization or it may be a new employee. Careful reflection on how their behaviour or responses impact you and the organization is necessary.

If you are a leader in your organization, you may have staff members coming to you to complain about someone else. At other times, multiple people on a team may challenge you or cause a general disturbance on the team. You hired these people believing them to be passionate visionaries capable of great things, yet during these times you question your judgment and wonder how you could have been so wrong.

Often times when we are faced by people that we see as disturbers in the workplace, our response is to become rigid and set up more rules, or to fire the person. If you find yourself in this situation, before you do anything, breathe. Take a minute. Shift your perspective and see how this situation might actually be an opportunity. Your careful response and reflection is required to be effective. When a disturber or multiple disturbers show up in an organization it is actually a sign that something in the system wants or needs change. Something that used to work is no longer working and someone is making us aware of this. It may not be spoken eloquently or nicely, but regardless, it is being spoken, and it is very important to listen. Most of the time when disturbers show up, we see them as the problem and we don't see the message that they bring. We feel threatened and concerned for the safety and well-being of our organization and other employees.

As we calmly and curiously approach the situation in a grounded way we obtain more information and the picture becomes clearer. Often disturbers are believed to be poisoning the organization and they are often treated as scapegoats. It is very important to notice if you are labeling the employee as the problem.

Notice your internal response to what is going on in the environment. Learn what the voice within you is trying to say. Whatever is invoked in you is likely also invoked in them. For example, if you feel powerless, chances are they feel the same way. See yourself as a mirror for what is going on with them.

The environment needs to be shifted to one of acceptance and full self expression. If someone comes to you with a complaint about another person, you will need to ensure that the situation is remedied as you do not want to collude with the complaint or complainer.

I was presenting for a corporate group and shared about the importance of knowing one's values (which is the information shared earlier in chapter five). While facilitating, there were a lot of different opinions about the values and vision of the group. Sometimes differing values can prevent openness and collaboration. When you are clear on your own values you have increased awareness regarding behaviours or attitudes which contradict them.

I asked the group to consider how they react to people who do not possess their same values. One participant shared that "The values I chose are exactly the values that I feel others should have. I notice that I get angry with people if they do not possess them." She later told me that because of the workshop, she learned that she has to accept that not everyone will have the same values as she has and she is learning to change the way she reacts. Hearing that feedback was incredibly positive! It was encouraging that instead of pointing blame outwards at others, this woman was willing to explore how her own beliefs were impacting how she was seeing and dealing with others.

It is sometimes difficult to deal with these types of situations alone, so you may want to consider consulting a facilitator skilled in team relationship systems coaching. The Center for Right Relationship (CRR) offers coaching to teams internationally (www.centerforrightrelationship. com). Coaches from this network are highly trained and can assist you to deal with challenges in a manner that will result in growth for your organization's vision and productivity. In addition, an executive leadership coach trained in assisting those in leadership positions may also be helpful.

## Your Environment

» How do people support and encourage one another?

» Is there a shared purpose in your organization and is there a sense of responsibility towards one another? How does this show up?

» Is the level of trust high? What tells you this?

» Are people encouraged to openly express ideas, disagreements and feelings?

» Is conflict viewed as an opportunity for growth? When it occurs how is conflict dealt with?

» Is the asking of questions and sharing of opinions encouraged?

» Is creativity encouraged? How?

» Is there a sense of excitement and adventure in the business environment?

» Is there a drive for team, knowing the results produced by teams have the potential to be superior to those of individuals?

» Is there clear leadership and high standards in the team and environment?

» Is there low turnover?

» Is there integrity?

» Is there a sense that the team hires the best people, and that prospective team members are waiting to be hired?

# The Top Four Behaviours That Doom Relationships

Relationship and leadership coach, Fernando Lopez (2008) references John Gottman (1999) and Douglas Stone et al (1999) in his article "Behaviours that Doom Relationships." Furthermore, acknowledgment is also given to the Center for Right Relationship for their contribution to the ideas noted in this section.

There are four toxic behaviours that are so lethal to relationships that marital therapist and relationship expert, John Gottman (1999) calls them the Four Horsemen of the Apocalypse. They are criticism; defensiveness; contempt; and stonewalling.

As you read the description of each of these behaviours notice which ones are present in your relationships and which show up on the teams you lead. Along with each behaviour, you will find some antidotes that neutralize their toxicity. If you are the recipient of a Horseman behaviour, respond mindfully using one of the skills presented earlier, or use one of the following antidotes.

When you respond in a mindful manner, you will notice that other people's behaviours shift also. Horseman behaviours often occur when people are feeling powerless within a situation. It might seem paradoxical, but when somebody is using a Horseman behaviour you need to guide he or she toward a position of power rather than making them feel even more powerless by responding with the same behaviour.

Focus on how you want to behave regardless of what the other person does or does not do. Learn which of the toxic behaviours most often arises for you in relationships. Learn to rein it in and ask for assistance from those people close to you to get a handle on this habit. Work together to talk about challenges before conflict arises.

Find ways to add positivity to your relationships. A "reservoir" of positivity will help deal with Horsemen when they show up. Having conversations about the things that work well in the team setting or in a relationship is a powerful way of creating positivity. Creating positivity and articulating what you appreciate about others may in fact be the most powerful Horsemen antidote you can use (Lopez, 2008).

Rehearse the antidotes you want to use ahead of time so that when you actually need them you know what to do.

# Horseman Behaviour 1: Blame/Criticism.

Criticism consists of attacking or focusing on the other person instead of their behaviour. Criticism adds some negative commentary regarding the other person's character or personality. For example, asking "What is wrong with you" will turn a comment into a criticism.

## Antidotes

» When receiving criticism, take the attitude that the person criticizing you is doing so because they care about what you do, not because they want to make you feel bad. It is their unskillful attempt to give you useful feedback. By holding this perspective, you will then be able to have a conversation with them about how they can present complaints and criticism in a more useful and acceptable manner to you.

» When you have a complaint, ensure that it is directed towards a specific behaviour.

» Turn complaints into requests: Instead of becoming defensive, state what it is you need.

» Problem solving, clarifying, and asking for what you need is very important.

» Use what is called an "I message"; a way of stating how you feel and asking for what you need without blame.

» Remember that requests are not demands.

» Don't make the situation personal.

» Focus on the changes necessary to take care of the issue at hand.

» Look at your contribution to the problem. Even if you truly believe that the other person had a bigger contribution, you will feel less powerless if you are aware of how you also contributed to the problem and what you can change about it.

» Apologize, even if, in your opinion, you weren't being critical, what counts is what the listener experienced. Remain curious about the impact of what you say and how you say it.

» Take responsibility for how your way of being and communicating impacts people. Be willing to learn about yourself from others' feedback.

## Horseman Behaviour 2: Defensiveness

Although it's understandable that you would defend yourself when criticized, research shows that this approach rarely works. A person who is presenting in an attacking manner does not typically back down or apologize. This is because defensiveness is really another way of blaming and it escalates the conflict. It is common for the defensive person to feel like he or she is above the conflict, when in fact, he or she is contributing to the conflict. However, if you try to point this out, it typically falls within a blind-spot (Lopez, 2008).

Question to consider: When do you react with defensiveness or fail to take responsibility for your contribution to problems?

### Antidotes

» If you are feeling defensive, repeat what you heard and ask for clarification. For example: "I'm hearing you say that I am not trustworthy. Can you clarify that?"

» Search for the "2%" truth in what you are hearing the other person say about you. For example: It is true that I often don't leave enough time for unpredictable delays and I can see how that would make me untrustworthy.

» If the other person is getting defensive:, ask them what they heard you say. It is quite possible that they misunderstood you or that they felt criticized without you being aware of it. Take responsibility for your impact and rephrase what you wanted to say.

» Show the other person that you respect and trust them and that their image is not at stake (assuming that is true). This will lower their defenses and you will have a more productive conversation.

» People get defensive when they don't feel heard so use active listening and I messages. Make sure you convey to the other person that you understand what he or she is saying.

## Horseman Behaviour 3: Contempt

Contempt includes sarcasm, belittling, cynicism, name-calling, hostile humor, and belligerence. Contempt is very damaging as it conveys disgust and condescension. It has been shown to be harmful to the physical health of an individual. Contempt is fueled by long-simmering negative thoughts about a person. You're more likely to have such thoughts if your differences are not regularly resolved after they occur.

Question to consider: When do you act contemptuously?

## Antidotes

» If another person is acting contemptuously, express your feelings, identify the unwanted behaviour, and try asking: "What is your intention in saying that?" They may not be aware that they sound contemptuous to you. Clarifying their intention will help to facilitate understanding.

» You can also ask: "Are you aware of your impact right now?" and explain your experience. Then ask, "Is it the impact you want to have?"

» Create a culture of kindness and admiration in your partnerships.

» Seek to understand others and acknowledge them first.

Your actions will be much more effective when they come from a place of respect rather than contempt. Constructive conflict is only possible from a basis of respect. Realize that respect is given, not earned. If you don't respect someone, it is about your inability to see the greatness, creativity, and resourcefulness in that person, not about that person's lower value as a human being. Stop any sarcasm, cynicism, name-calling, and belligerence as it is harming your relationships more than you think.

# Horseman Behaviour 4: Stonewalling

Stonewalling includes cutting off communication, silent treatments, refusals to engage, withdrawal, and being reluctant to express directly what you are thinking.

Question to consider: What areas do you avoid talking about?

## Antidotes

- » If you are triggered, find a way to self-soothe. Do you have a meditation or relaxation practice?
- » Reflect on the practices given throughout this book to assist you in dealing with triggers and with stonewalling behaviour.
- » Look at your fear of speaking; what information is it giving you? What part of your identity is at stake? Get grounded in who you really are before speaking.
- » Differentiate between fear and any actual danger involved if you say something. If there is actual danger, you don't want to expose yourself to it, but it may be useful to explain the reason for withholding the information.

» What safety conditions can you design with the other person so that you (or they) are better able to speak directly? Perhaps you can set a specific time to talk, establish confidentiality about what is spoken, and meet at a neutral place. If the other person is stonewalling you, take a look at what you are doing that makes him not feel safe expressing himself. Do you feel contempt? Have you not valued their ideas in the past? Have you been judgmental?

» People sometimes don't know how to communicate effectively. Use REAP and GREAT goals to assist you to stay on track. Help educate others on effective communication and model an approach that is patient, kind, direct and honest.

# When Challenges Arise: How to Bring Forward Positivity and Productivity

## 16

Building trust and using a specific form of questioning called appreciative inquiry provide two avenues for dealing with challenges on teams.

## Building Trust

To be an effective leader you must focus on building trust. In order to build an environment of trust, you can consider the following questions and see how you can apply them to your environment. Think about all the teams you've been on and find one specific experience that exemplifies an environment of trust.

- » What were the qualities of that team that enhanced trust?
- » What did you bring to the table that helped?
- » What were the benefits of this environment of trust?
    - » To team members?
    - » To the work they were doing?
    - » To their organization?
- » What can you learn from this team that might help your current team build a stronger environment of trust?
- » What can you bring forward yourself from that experience to assist you with your current situation?

## Appreciative Inquiry (AI)

AI is a process of questioning for facilitating strategic change in organizations. AI questions focus on what is going well, what you would like more of and will assist you and others to grow in areas that are important to you. AI explores stories of life-giving forces, creates shared images and dreams for a preferred future, and finds the positive in situations.

Questions from the field of AI can be used to assist you with difficult situations or when a saboteur that is preventing you, or others, from reaching your goals. Focused questions invite people to elaborate further on disappointments, gaps, and unmet expectations – the root causes that lead to breakdowns. Furthermore, outcomes of AI interventions show that when people engage in a search for life-giving moments and exceptional moments of meaning that creative imagination and bonds between people also grow (Rothwell & Sullivan, 2005).

As you explore a challenge you face in your leadership, consider the following questions:

» What makes me most proud of my work?
» When did this organization feel most "alive" and happy?
» What would it look like if it felt this way again?
» How can I and others begin to re-create this reality?
» When were things at their best?
» What contributed to this positive experience?

# Mindfulness & Action

Although the two terms mindfulness and action may seem contradictory, it is with action that we make mindfulness activities a priority in our lives.

By revealing how unconscious activities may or may not be producing the results you desire in your life, and through the use of a few simple exercises you can transform your life and the lives of people around you.

Consider what an individual action plan for applying mindfulness in your life and work might look like. This action plan may involve initiating mindfulness based activities on your own, or in a group.

The practices that follow are intended to help you feel grounded, to clear your mind, and are designed to assist you in getting in touch with what is important to you. There are many ways to become mindful and grounded; you can use visualization or meditation, you can focus on your breath, or you can use movement, dance, yoga, or art. You can also become more mindful by writing affirmations, or by establishing an intention for the day and writing it down.

As you read the following exercises, consider which activities might be good for you to include in a daily or weekly routine and which exercises might be good for your team to practice as a group. Do not rush through these exercises. Try one each day, or, try the same exercise every day for a week. Each exercise has a purpose so stick with it and see what difference it makes in your life.

## Create a Daily Intention

In your mind, create an intention for the day. This might be a practice of being present in the moment, being at peace, or being loving towards others. Any intention you create is perfect.

The intention I am creating for today is to be empowered, inspirational and non-attached to outcome. Wait and see what unfolds as you bring your intention forward into the day.

For example: Today I am creating a day and life of love and peacefulness.

Or: Acceptance, gratitude, presence, or whatever fits for you!

As you go about your day, don't force anything to happen, just BE. Be watchful for your intention showing up in your world; this is living with awareness.

The intention I am creating for today is:

_____

_____

Think back to how you started your day this morning. Did you roll out of bed, or did you eagerly jump out of bed excited and inspired about the day? What thoughts were you saying to yourself as your eyes opened and you began your day? If you are unsure or curious regarding what those awaking thoughts were and how they shaped your day, write yourself a note to consciously reflect on whatever arises the moment you awake tomorrow morning.

Thoughts that arise at waking often shed light on direction, paths, intuitions, dreams and goals. They may also be indicators that you are not living in line with what you say you are committed to in your life, or they may give you clear indicators that you are.

In order to explore your thoughts, take a pen and paper and write non-stop for ten minutes about anything that is in your mind. This is called flow writing; it is uncensored and unfiltered and is only for your eyes. When you write non-stop in this manner, you gain clarity and insight.

You will likely find that when you do this exercise what you initially write is insignificant. Although you can do this practice anytime you may find that doing it consistently is helpful.

## Presence Through Breath

Set aside a time everyday for just being; it could be five, ten or fifteen minutes, and focus on being fully present.

Keep your posture upright and grounded. Sit up tall and place your feet flat on the floor. Close your eyes and take some deep breaths. Begin by breathing out through your mouth, and after a few times, breath in and out through your nose only. Bring your attention to the breath as it leaves your nose and as it enters your nose. Keep your mind focused on your nose, and any time you notice your mind wandering, bring the focus gently back to the sensation on your nose. If you find your attention wanders bring it back to the sensation.

Now count to twenty focusing on the inhale and then count to twenty focusing on the exhale.

Alternately you can also use opposite nostril breathing to help you focus and to clear your mind. In this practice, you place you thumb on your right nostril and your fourth finger from the same hand on your left nostril. You then breathe in counting to four through the right, keeping the left blocked, and then release the left, exhaling through it (counting to four) and as you do so, you block the right. Next, inhale in through the left, keeping the right blocked. Release the right and exhale, covering the left as you do so. Carry on in this manner for ten rounds.

## Presence Through Reflection

Think of a time when you were able to stay in the present moment when others around you were in turmoil or were experiencing stress.

» What was this situation?

» How did you stay present and in the moment?

» What were the results?

» How can your ability to be in the present moment help your team to be more effective right now?

» Imagine a world where people are fully present and living in the moment.

» How would people be acting?

» What would leadership be like?

In order to take steps towards exuding a positive vibration, you need to get in touch with the things that bring you joy. As you become a more joyful and fulfilled leader, others will want to live with the same energy and passion that you have. People who exude joy cause curiosity in others. In order to manifest abundance, it is helpful to operate at a vibrational level where people say, "I want what that person has!" When you become more joyful others will sense this and may ask you questions like, "What are you doing lately? You look very happy! Are you in love? What's new, or what changes have you made? You look different."

One way of moving toward joy is by taking a few minutes at the end of any given day and reflecting on the events of that day.

Take a piece of paper and draw a line down the middle. On the left side note all of the things that left you feeling positive and inspired and brought you great joy, on the right side of the page write down the events or situations that left you feeling drained or uninspired.

| Moving Towards JOY | Moving Away From JOY |
|---|---|
| | |

Pay attention to the things that you have written down that will assist you in living your best life! After having used this list to record your daily events, you can create a new list that reflects the things you enjoy doing that bring you great joy. You may also add things you did as a child that you purely enjoyed.

Feel free to replicate this chart and use it on a daily basis to reflect on your day and to find more joy! What happened today that inspired you and that brought you joy?

_____

_____

Create those opportunities if they are missing. List one thing that you will do to bring joy into your life today:

_____

_____

## Guided Visualization

Let yourself settle into a comfortable sitting posture and check that you're sitting evenly, so your weight falls equally on the left and right sides of your body. Extending awareness into your body, deeply inhale and exhale a few times so that you can feel the chest and the ribcage opening – feel your shoulders and arms lifting slightly on the inward breath – and on the out-breath, allowing them to roll back slightly.

Let your breath return to normal and as you do this let your shoulders relax so that your chest remains more open. Adjust your hands on your lap to keep this openness in your chest. Let your spine be upright – relaxed, not rigid. Allow your head to relax evenly at the top of your spine.

Relax your eyes – relax your shoulders – relax your stomach. Now experience your breath as it comes naturally into your body and goes out again.

Visualize a colour that represents healing and imagine it entering into your body. Gently direct that colour so it fills your body and any areas in need of healing. Imagine that you have an abundance of healing energy. See the healing colour fill you to overflowing and visualize it reaching people, places and situations that are important to you.

There are many things to be grateful for, and often times we focus on what is missing in our lives rather than what is present. As you read this, take a moment and give thanks for something that you are thankful for.

In this practice you are shifting your attention from self-centered thinking to seeing things as they are, for there is wisdom and liberation in seeing how you act and the impact of these actions on others.

Close your eyes, sit with a tall spine, focus and ground yourself, bring attention to your breath. What you have received today? Go through your day's events and notice what you have given to others. Be as specific and concrete as possible.

Now consider what difficulties and troubles did I cause today? Have the courage to look at how you may have intentionally or unintentionally caused another person difficulty.

Extend thoughts of loving kindness to anyone you may have intentionally or unintentionally harmed. Close your eyes and reflecting on all the things that you are grateful for at this moment and give thanks for small blessings. (Exercise adapted from Grounded in Gratitude, *Yoga Journal*, Boccio, 2006).

## Connecting With Your Heart

Look back over your life and think of two good deeds you have done. Be aware of how these memories affect your consciousness (how they transform the state of your heart and mind). Recall them anytime you are having a difficult time and need to focus on well-being and abundance.

Take some time and write down the things that you have done that you are proud of in your life.

*By becoming increasingly mindful, leaders become more in tune with their intuition and as a result, become more compassionate, non-blaming, and respectful. As stated earlier in this book, there are many examples from our own personal lives and from situations around the world where we look to the other person to change, to be different, to give us what we want, and mostly, to stop being so difficult. The invitation and solution lies in looking at our role in the interaction and dynamic, owning it, and responding responsibly. By modeling these behaviours, you will inspire others to also rise to the challenge of personal responsibility and reflection. Practice mindfulness and self-reflection often and you will experience the difference that it makes.*

*Acknowledge your own accomplishments. Congratulate yourself on having the courage to take the steps necessary to become a conscious mindful leader. Appreciate yourself!*

# References

Bernhut, S. (2002). "Leader's Edge With Daniel Goleman," *Ivey Business Journal*. Toronto: Ivey management services.

Boccio, F. (2006). Grounded in Gratitude. *Yoga Journal*, 199, 113-116.

Bogo, M. (1993). The student/field instructor relationship: The critical factor in field education. *The Clinical Supervisor II* (2): 23-36.

Cameron, J. (1992). *The artist's way*. New York: Penguin Putnam Inc.

Cameron, J. (2002). *The artist's way at work*. New York: Penguin Putnam Inc.

Caspi, J & W. Reid. (2002). *Educational supervision in social work: A task centered model for field Instruction and staff development*. Columbia University Press: New York.

Cherney, J., Whitney, D., & Trosten-Bloom, A. (2004). *Appreciative team building: Positive questions to bring out the best of your team*. Lincoln, NE: iUniverse, Inc.

Conchie, B (2008). *The seven demands of executive leadership* Available: http://gmj.gallup.com/content/11614/default.aspx

Covey, S. ( 1990). *The 7 Habits of highly effective people*. New York: Simon Schuster, Inc.

Covey, S. ( 2004). *The 8th Habit: From effectiveness to greatness*. New York: Free Press.

Downs, M. F. (2006). *Between us: Growing relational possibilities in clinical supervision*. Stone Center: Wellesley, MA.

Ellison, M. L. (1994). Critical Field instructor behaviours: Student field instructor views. *Arete* 18 (2): 12-21.

Epstein, M. (1995). *Thoughts without a thinker: Psychotherapy from a Buddhist Perspective*. New York: Basic Books.

Gilbreath, B., & Benson, P. G. (2004). The contribution of supervisor behaviour to employee psychological well-being. *Work and Stress*, 18, 255-266.

Goleman, D. (1995). *Emotional intelligence: Why it can matter more than IQ*. New York: Bantam Books.

Goleman, D., Boyatzis, R., & McKee, A. (2002). *Primal leadership: Realizing the power of emotional intelligence*. Cambridge: Harvard Business Press.

Gottman, J. (1999). *Seven principles for making marriage work*. New York: Three Rivers Press.

Gizykski, M. (1978). Self-awareness of the supervisor in supervision. *Clinical Social Work* Journal 6: 202-210.

Huber, C (1990). *That which you are seeking is causing you to seek*. California: Keep it simple.

Ipsos Reid (2008a). One in three canadian workers say they're dragged down by a negative atmosphere at work. Available at: http://www.ipsos-na.com/news/pressrelease.cfm?id=4128

Ipsos Reid (2008b). Americans find simple expressions of appreciation to be the most meaningful. Available at: http://www.ipsos-na.com/news/pressrelease.cfm?id=4211

Kornfield, J. (1993). *A path with heart*. Bantam Books: New York.

Kadushin, A. E. (1992). *Supervision in social work*. New York: Columbia University Press.

Latting, J. L. (1992). Giving corrective feedback: A decisional analysis. *Social Work 37(5)*: 424-430.

Lee, C. ( 2004). *Yoga Body: Buddha Mind*. New York: Riverhead Books.

Lopez, F. (2008). *The top four behaviours that doom relationships*. ORSC global coaching network. Information available at: http://www.bridgespace.ca

Randstad 2008 *Outlook Report*, Montreal.

Richo, D ( 2002). *How to be an adult in relationships: The five keys to mindful loving.* Boston: Shambhala.

Rothwell, W..& Sullivan, R. 2005). *Practicing Organization Development: A guide.* San Francisco: Pfeiffer.

Segal, Z., Williams, J., & J. Teasdale ( 2002). *Mindfulness Based Cognitive Therapy for Depression.* New York: Guilford Press.

Siegel, D. (1999). *The developing mind: How relationships and the brain interact to shape who we are.* New York: Guilford Press.

Siegel, D. (2007). *The mindful brain: Reflection and attunement in the cultivation of well-being.* New York: WW Norton and Co.

Siegel, D. & Hartzell, M. (2004). *Parenting from the Inside Out.* New York: Penguin Group (USA) Inc.

Stone, D., & Patton, B. (1999). *Difficult Conversations.* New York: Penguin Putnam Inc.

Wheatley, M. (2007). *Leadership and the new science: Discovering order in a chaotic world (3rd Ed.).* San Francisco: Berrett-Koehler Publishers, Inc.

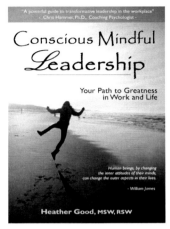

# Share
# Conscious Mindful
# Leadership
## with Colleagues, Managers and Other Leaders

Drawing upon the most current research in mindfulness, attachment and emotional intelligence, *Conscious Mindful Leadership* assists individuals and teams to increase awareness and relatedness in the workplace. Leaders will find employees thriving and showing increased results and commitment to their jobs and goals.

**If you are interested in having workshops based on**
*Conscious Mindful Leadership* **offered for your organization**
**or to order copies of the book:**

**Good Coaching**
**Email: heather@goodcoaching.ca**
**Or visit www.goodcoaching.ca**

Discounts are available for orders of more than 25 books.

_____ (# of copies) **Conscious Mindful Leadership**        **$22.95**

Payable via company cheque.

Payable in Canadian funds. GST, postage and handling will be applied to each order.

Company: _____

Name: _____

Order online and submit payment via PayPal.

Address: _____

City: _____ Prov: _____

Postal Code: _____

Daytime Phone: ( _____ ) _____

Signature: _____